Who Are the Seventh-day Adventists?

(A Brief Look at Their History, Beliefs, People, Church, and Mission)

JOHN SEAMAN

REVIEW AND HERALD® PUBLISHING ASSOCIATION
HAGERSTOWN, MD 21740

This book was
Edited by Richard W. Coffen
Copyedited by Jocelyn Fay and James Cavil
Designed by Reger Smith, Jr.
Cover photos by PhotoDisc
Typeset: 9/13 Stone Informal

PRINTED IN U.S.A.

05 04 5 4 3

R&H Cataloging Service
Seaman, John G. 1963-
Who are the Seventh-day Adventists?

1. Seventh-day Adventists. I. Title.

286.732

ISBN 0-8280-1350-0

Contents

5	Before You Begin . . .	
7	**Chapter 1**	Where Did the Seventh-day Adventists Come From?
16	**Chapter 2**	What Do Seventh-day Adventists Believe?
22	**Chapter 3**	What Are the People Like?
28	**Chapter 4**	What Is the Seventh-day Adventist Church Like?
35	**Chapter 5**	What Is the Seventh-day Adventist Mission?
42	Before You Finish . . .	
44	**Appendix A**	A Brief Scriptural Summary of Selected Seventh-day Adventist Beliefs
50	**Appendix B**	27 Fundamental Beliefs of Seventh-day Adventists

Before You Begin . . .

IF YOU WOULD ASK 100 people on the street the question Who are the Seventh-day Adventists? you would probably get responses ranging from the humorous to the absurd to the inaccurate. Replies might include (which I've heard through the years):

"I think they're a rock group."

"Aren't they the people who don't believe in Jesus?"

"They don't believe in the Bible. They have some prophet they follow."

"Aren't those the people who eat only vegetables and soybeans?"

"They're legalists. They believe you're saved by the good works you do."

"I think they have something to do with the Jewish people."

"Stay away from them. I hear they're a cult!"

We certainly cannot blame these people for their candid responses, because they probably have never taken the time to learn who Seventh-day Adventist Christians really are. They may never have read a book outlining what Seventh-day Adventists stand for and what their beliefs are. But those simple statements, however candid, certainly reflect who Seventh-day Adventists are *not*.

So who *are* they really? Are Seventh-day Adventists some strange group with weird ideas? Do their members live in communes? Do their leaders make bizarre predictions about the future? Or are they an assembly of Christians with a message and lifestyle that might be worth a closer look?

As we begin this study together, it's my hope that you'll get a clearer picture of Seventh-day Adventists and their convictions. Then you'll be able to make an intelligent decision for yourself. At this point you can pat yourself on the back for going right to the source and not taking the word of the "experts" on the street.

CHAPTER 1

Where Did the Seventh-day Adventists Come From?

"MOMMY, WHERE DID I COME FROM?" The question can strike terror in the hearts of unprepared parents, or it can bring a smile to the faces of those who have been waiting for an inquisitive youngster to raise it.

Where did we come from? It's a question that has been debated in lecture halls and universities, and by great philosophers. People want to know where they came from and why they're here. So the debates continue.

Where did the Seventh-day Adventists come from? History records many great organizations and movements that were created almost overnight, but this was not the case with the Seventh-day Adventist Church. Rather than being an immediate creation, the church was formed by a progressive series of historical events. Through much study its pioneers came to a deeper understanding of Scripture.

Seventh-day Adventism's historical roots go all the way back to William Miller, who was born February 15, 1782, in Pittsfield, Massachusetts. Raised in a religious home in northern New York State, Miller was the oldest of 16 children. As a child he was regularly loaded into a hard-case buggy and pulled to church by the family horse. His grandfather and two uncles served as Baptist ministers.

When he was 30 years old, Miller achieved the status of captain in the War of 1812. He was brilliant and well read but had become disenchanted with the Christianity of his childhood and so had chosen to adopt deism. This popular philosophy of the time claimed that God had no genuine, personal involvement in the affairs of our world. It taught that He had simply set the world in space and left it to its own devising.

After honorably serving his country, Miller returned to his farmhouse in Low Hampton, New York. As one might expect, deism didn't ultimately satisfy the longing in his heart for real meaning in life. Sometimes he attended the local Baptist church, but he still had deep questions within his heart.

In 1816 he quietly began a thorough, systematic investigation of Scripture. He studied on his own, without the help of religious teachers, using his Bible and a Cruden's concordance to look up texts for comparison. His initial interest in prophecy led him to discover Bible truths that differed from the popular opinions of the day. However, these truths actually seemed minor in comparison to the conclusion that he reached after two years of meticulous study. He came to the stunning conclusion that Jesus Christ would return around the year 1843, about 25 years hence. (The date was subsequently revised until October 22, 1844, was settled on.)

This major conviction, the soon coming of Christ, radically departed from the common consensus. Popular teaching insisted that there would be 1,000 years of peace and happiness in the world *before* Christ returned to earth. Being aware of this teaching, Miller went back to his deliberation to make sure he was correct in his assumptions. The more he studied, the more convinced he became.

On August 13, 1831, this 49-year-old farmer felt the strong conviction that he should share his biblical discoveries. He slowly made his way to a private grove of trees, where he knelt in prayer and wrestled with his overwhelming conviction. He wasn't a preacher. He didn't want to preach. Finally, to settle the turmoil in his soul, Miller made a deal with God. He promised God that if someone should invite him to preach, he would. However, he wouldn't solicit any speaking engagements. He left the grove confident: Who would ask a farmer, unschooled in religious thought, to preach?

Miller returned to his house and relaxed in his living room. About 30 minutes later he heard the sound of a horse's hooves clopping up the road. Soon Irving Guilford, Miller's nephew, was knocking on the oak door. Irving had but one purpose in mind—to invite Miller to share his biblical views with the Dresden Baptist Church, seven miles away. Miller reluctantly agreed to go preach, keeping the promise he'd made with God in the grove.

And Miller didn't stop preaching! During the next 13 years Miller preached 4,000 times, in at least 500 towns. More than 200 clergy accepted his views on Christ's soon coming, and estimates of the number of believers who agreed with him range from 50,000 to 100,000. These followers of Miller's views were—and are—often referred to as "Millerites." This extraordinary sequence of events is recorded in history as the Millerite movement.

What was Miller's message? It was the simple interpretation of a prophetic chapter in Scripture. Taking the prophecy found in Daniel 8:14, which said: "Unto two thousand and three hundred days; then shall the sanctuary be cleansed," Miller applied the biblical principle that in prophecy a day can symbolize one year. According to Miller, the 2300 days spoken of in Daniel meant 2300 years.

Miller wasn't the first student of Scripture to arrive at such a conclusion. Records show that a number of other Bible scholars, centuries before Miller, held to the belief that these biblical time prophecies referred to years, not literal days. One of the most notable was Sir Isaac Newton. In addition to investigating the laws of gravity, he was fascinated with Bible prophecy and wrote much on the subject.

In the early nineteenth century the understanding of how to interpret the time prophecies of the Bible was widespread. Many teachers of God's Word believed that some fulfillment of the 2300 days spoken of in Daniel would soon take place.

Through biblical and historical study, Miller was

able to determine the starting date for the 2300-day prophecy as 457 B.C. When adding 2,300 years to this date, he ultimately concluded that October 22, 1844, would be the date for the cleansing of the sanctuary.*

In the popular religious thinking of Miller's day, the term *sanctuary* represented the world. And how else could the world be cleansed but by fire? And if the world was going to be cleansed by fire, then it must mean that Jesus was going to come!

You can imagine the excitement of the Millerites! Those who believed Miller eagerly awaited the coming of the Lord on October 22, 1844. There were those who had lost loved ones just months, weeks, and even days before. They waited with eager expectation to see them again. But Jesus didn't return as Miller and his followers expected. Needless to say, the Millerites endured great disappointment. Some left the movement, starting their own churches. Others abandoned Miller's ideas altogether and returned to their former places of worship. Some Millerites were so wrapped up in the sensationalism of the movement that they wouldn't listen to anything else Miller subsequently said.

This sudden dramatic turn of events dealt a hard blow to Miller. He had never intended that the movement be anything more than a search for truth. He had suffered scorn and ridicule while presenting his teachings. He had listened to the scoffers and had seen the cartoons mocking his message. But now his own friends had deserted him.

However, a small group was trying to obey the Word of God and continue the search for truth. These "former" Millerites went back to the study of the Bible and saw where Miller had made his errors. The dating had indeed been correct, they concluded, but the assumptions about what would happen had been wrong. After renewed study of Scripture, they were even more convinced than ever that Jesus was coming soon, but they were equally certain that the actual date of His coming could not be determined. They discovered there would not be 1,000 years of peace *before* Jesus' arrival. They believed instead that the world would become increasingly wicked and that Jesus would come to put an end to the unchecked sin in the world. Then the millennium spoken of in the last book of the New Testament would begin.

As the small group of Bible students discovered that Miller was correct in his chronological conclusions, but wrong in the event, they also uncovered other truths in the process. One of these affirmations was their rediscovery of the biblical Sabbath—the seventh day of the week. The seventh-day Sabbath had been kept by different groups and individuals since Creation, but now it was unearthed in the context of Christ's second advent.

Joseph Bates, a retired sea captain who had enjoyed an adventurous and active career, was one of the early Sabbathkeepers who also believed in the soon coming of Jesus. He actively promoted his views regarding the biblical Sabbath and served as a member of the committee that would call for the first "Advent General Conference."

Many other Adventist "pioneers" sought further truth from God's Word during the mid-1800s.

Hiram Edson's study of Scripture led him to understand where Miller had made his errors in biblical interpretation and thus why Christ hadn't returned in 1844. He saw that the sanctuary Miller preached about did not represent the earth but rather referred to the ministry of Jesus in heaven. Edson found evidence from the Bible that Christ had indeed begun a new phase of His ministry and the prophecy had, therefore, been fulfilled!

As many struggled with their disappointment following October 22, 1844, God chose to give them encouragement through a 17-year-old girl, Ellen Harmon. While praying with a small group of friends in Portland, Maine, she felt God's power and presence in vision. She saw that they truly were on the right path of Bible study and that as long as they kept their focus on Jesus, He would lead and guide them. She shared what she had seen with others, who were indeed encouraged. One of those who heard her was a young preacher named James White. He and Ellen eventually married, and together they exerted a strong influence in the establishment of the Seventh-day Adventist Church.

In late 1846 James and Ellen White began keeping the seventh-day Sabbath themselves. They, along with Joseph Bates and Hiram Edson, led out in studying Scripture and promoting their doctrinal understanding based on God's Word. They were not alone, of course. Hundreds of others were likewise sharing what they had learned. In 1848 the first "Sabbath Conference" was convened in Rocky Hill, Connecticut. It offered a time of prayer and Bible study.

As belief in the lasting importance of the biblical Sabbath grew, so did the need to share it with others. Several papers and magazines were published, among them the *Second Advent Review and Sabbath Herald,* whose first issue was published in 1849. (This periodical continues as the weekly *Adventist Review.*) In 1853 Sabbath schools, patterned after Sunday schools (which had become popular in America in 1791), were organized in the Adventist churches.

As the group of those who believed the Sabbath and the Second Coming grew, it became apparent that they could carry out their mission more efficiently if they would organize. The first organizational step would be to pick a name for this growing movement. After many names were discussed, the appellation Seventh-day Adventist was chosen. It clearly described the denomination—those who keep the seventh-day Sabbath and look forward to Jesus' soon coming.

In 1863 delegates from the various "conferences" assembled together in Michigan and voted a list of officers to oversee the new denomination. The attendees asked James White to serve as president, but he turned down the nomination. John Byington, a former Wesleyan pastor, was then elected as the first president of the General Conference of Seventh-day Adventists. The organizational process was pretty much complete.

Miller didn't discover all the truth that needed to be found, but he did take a giant step forward in understanding of the Bible. Miller's teachings helped to change the religious landscape forever. Millions of people today, across denominational lines, believe we cannot expect 1,000 years of peace before Jesus comes. Many churches also teach that the world is getting too wicked and will end soon. Is that so unusual? Well, it is if you realize that before William Miller began his preaching, you might have been disfellowshipped from your church for saying that Jesus was coming soon. Those who believe in the soon coming of Jesus are today called Adventists. So in some respect, there are many "Adventists" in churches across the world today. They owe a thank-you to William Miller for his study of Scripture.

This has been an abbreviated history of the formation of the Seventh-day Adventist Church. In 1863, at its formation, there were only 3,500 baptized members and 30 pastors. Today the denomination has a membership of more than 13 million, with churches dotting the globe, and continues to grow by more than 1 million members every year.

What lies behind the rapid growth of the Seventh-day Adventist denomination? What common beliefs tie its membership, crossing cultural and racial and ethnic lines? Let's take a moment to look at that now in chapter 2.

---

*The starting point of the 2300-day prophecy was the decree given by Persian King Artaxerxes for Israel to return to Jerusalem and rebuild their city. He issued the decree in 457 B.C. Further investigation revealed that the exact date for the decree was the tenth day of the seventh Jewish month (the ancient Hebrew Day of Atonement). When adding 2,300 years to 457 B.C., one arrives at the date A.D. 1844. (There is no zero year in the transition between B.C. and A.D.)

CHAPTER 2

What Do Seventh-day Adventists Believe?

RALPH WALDO EMERSON ONCE WROTE, "We are born believing. A man bears beliefs, as a tree bears apples." He was pretty much right! Sure, maybe we don't come laden with opinions and beliefs from the womb, but we gain them quickly and remain opinionated until we gasp our last breath. Beliefs help to shape the way we live and respond to the world around us. Some beliefs we pick up during our infancy, whereas we acquire others during the course of a lifetime.

Why are beliefs so important? Because what we believe plays an important role in how we act. If you believe your mother-in-law is coming for dinner, you'll adjust your plans and prepare your house accordingly. If you believe you're old enough to drive a car, you'll drop subtle (maybe not-so-subtle) hints to your mom or dad to convince them of the same. If you believe children should make a positive contribution to the maintenance of the household, you'll withhold allowances or other privileges if they become lax in carrying out their responsibilities.

In today's society it appears that the number of beliefs held in common has greatly diminished. Individual opinions have replaced community values. Even among (and within) religious denominations a wide variety of views compete for acceptance.

The Seventh-day Adventist denomination is made up of individuals. Each person has different ideas, different ways of doing things, and different ways of saying things. But even within such diversity, strong common threads of belief run through every Seventh-day Adventist's heart. It's what makes the church unique. Around the world, from Pakistan to Peru, from Cambodia to Canada, from Sweden to South Africa, from the Ukraine to the United States, these common threads bind the church together. Using Scripture as their guide, members have formed an understanding of what God wants them to believe and how He wants them to translate those beliefs into responsible action.

The following offers a brief summary of certain main tenets of faith held in common by Seventh-day Adventists, regardless of where they live. (For a more detailed discussion of Seventh-day Adventist beliefs, please refer to the appendices.)

The Authority of God and Scripture—Seventh-day Adventists believe that the Holy Scriptures reveal God's will and constitute the foundation for all belief. Seventh-day Adventists believe in the unity and eternal existence of the Godhead; the Godhead being comprised of Father, Son, and Holy Spirit.

The Salvation of Humanity—Seventh-day Adventists believe that man and woman were made perfect moral beings at Creation. However, they sinned. As a result, the perfect world God desired for them was marred. We are all born now as sinful beings and in need of a Saviour.

Seventh-day Adventists believe that Jesus Christ came to this world, lived a sinless life, was crucified on Calvary for our sins, and rose again a victorious Saviour. Jesus offers His free gift of grace to all those who will accept it. Seventh-day Adventists believe it is impossible to do good works as a means of being saved; instead, good works are a natural, loving response to God's gift of salvation.

The "Great Controversy" Theme—Seventh-day Adventists believe that Lucifer, an angel whom God originally created perfect, rebelled in heaven. Lucifer was cast out of heaven, along with the angels that chose to side with him. Now called Satan, he attempts to persuade as many human beings as possible to follow his way. He continues a massive campaign to try to destroy God's credibility with the universe. Satan accuses God of establishing laws that are unjust. God created a morally perfect world, but Satan has often succeeded in persuading humans to go against God's authority and give in to the immoral attractions of sin.

The Scriptures describe the fall and restoration of humanity. They also reveal God's plan to restore Planet Earth for the benefit of those who have accepted His gift of grace and have demonstrated obedience to Him.

Final Prophetic Events—Seventh-day Adventists believe that Jesus is in heaven, actively representing the human race, enabling as many who will to be reunited with Him. As evidenced in their name, Seventh-day Adventists believe in the soon coming of Jesus. They believe that the Second Advent will be a literal event visibly seen by all earth dwellers.

Seventh-day Adventists believe that those who during their lives accepted Jesus Christ as their Saviour but have since died will be resurrected at Christ's second coming. Jesus will once again give them the breath of life. Thus the dead are not now alive in heaven but remain in their graves until the resurrection. The coming of Jesus will also be the starting point of the 1,000-year period spoken of in Scripture and commonly referred to as the millennium.

At the end of the millennium God will put a final end to sin and those who have chosen to follow its course. They will be destroyed, and the curse of sin will cease to exist. Then Jesus will re-create the world in its formerly perfect condition. His people will be able to live on the earth according to God's original plan.

Church Life—Seventh-day Adventists believe in church organization and encourage Christian fellowship. Upon acceptance of Jesus as personal Saviour and baptism, a person is welcomed into the fellowship of the Seventh-day Adventist Church. Seventh-day Adventists believe in baptism by immersion, following the example given by Jesus.

The church members have a common goal—to prepare people to meet the Lord. This purpose is accomplished by public and personal Bible study, daily sharing in the workplace, and always seeking to demonstrate the love of Christ by meeting the needs of people.

Seventh-day Adventists believe that God grants spiritual gifts to those individuals who willingly serve Him. They believe that the influence of all the gifts of the Spirit will be experienced in the church right up until the coming of Jesus. These gifts include the gift of prophecy, an especially essential gift for the end-time, according to Scripture.

Seventh-day Adventists weekly meet together for worship, and quarterly celebrate the Lord's Supper in remembrance of Christ's sacrifice on Calvary. They support the mission of the church by contributing tithe and freewill offerings.

Christian Life—Seventh-day Adventists believe that as Christians, their lifestyle should properly represent Jesus Christ. They carefully consider their actions, dress, choice of entertainment, and every other aspect of daily living. They strongly support family and the institution of marriage, which God originated in the Garden of Eden.

Seventh-day Adventists believe that their bodies have been entrusted to them by God. They follow biblical principles in caring for their bodies with proper nutrition and exercise and by maintaining other habits that contribute to good health.

The Sabbath—Seventh-day Adventists firmly believe in the authority of Scripture and so respect the laws that God has given in His Word. They uphold the Ten Commandments, including the commandment in which God says: "Remember the Sabbath day, to keep it holy." They believe that the Sabbath was given to the human race in the Garden of Eden at Creation and is still pertinent today. They find no evidence in the Bible that God ever changed His law. Thus Seventh-day Adventists attend church on Saturday, the seventh day of the week, and follow the scriptural guidelines for keeping the Sabbath holy.

The belief in the seventh day (Saturday) as the Sabbath is probably one of the more distinctive doctrines of the denomination. This doctrinal emphasis has helped to bring all nationalities, races, and ethnic groups together in worshiping the Lord of the Sabbath. People have become Seventh-day Adventists from many different backgrounds, joining together to worship on Saturday as a visible expression of their love for God and their acceptance of His authority in the universe and in their lives.

These beliefs, which all Seventh-day Adventists hold in common, have helped to keep the church united around the world.

As you read this brief summary, you may have discovered that some of the tenets mentioned are convictions that you hold too. This isn't unusual, because Seventh-day Adventists are also Christians. All Christians hold some fundamental doctrines in common.

Are Seventh-day Adventists different from everybody else? How can you spot a Seventh-day Adventist? How will Adventists act in their everyday life?

Let's take a moment to look at that in chapter 3.

CHAPTER 3

What Are the People Like?

IN 1972 *LIFE* MAGAZINE CHANGED from a weekly edition to a monthly one. Soon after the transition, subscribers began to lose interest, so on February 25, 1974, Time Incorporated placed a new magazine into circulation. Its title was plain but telling—*People*. Since its inception, *People* has sold hundreds of millions of copies. The magazine's simple format has always remained the same—print lots of pictures of people and stories about their lives.

People are fascinated with each other. Home video shows, real-life stories, and tabloid journalism have all carved out a niche in society. Perhaps the fascination comes because individuals make up society, and as social creatures we're curious to find out more about other people and what they're doing.

So who are the people that make up the Seventh-day Adventist Church? Are they ordinary people? Do they look the same as everyone else?

If I asked you to tell me what color it is outside,

you'd glance out your window and see a variety of colors—blue sky, brown dirt, green grass, red roses, white clouds. What color is it out there? The same analogy is true in trying to describe what a Seventh-day Adventist looks like. As with any other group, you cannot pigeonhole the people into a single category. Each member of the denomination is unique and has a special, personal contribution to make to the church. However, Seventh-day Adventists do share a lot of similar characteristics.

Seventh-day Adventist Christians believe they are sinners saved by God's unlimited grace—an important point to remember. They do *not* believe that they are faultless, that they are the only people going to heaven, or that they are better than anyone else. They believe they are sinners in need of a loving Saviour. So when you visit a Seventh-day Adventist church anywhere in the world, you'll find a warm group of people who will welcome you into their fellowship. They realize that all people are priceless in God's eyes.

Whether you meet Seventh-day Adventists in church, at the grocery store, on an airplane, or in the workplace, you might find them eager to share something about their church with you! As you've already discovered, some beliefs the Seventh-day Adventist Church teaches aren't taught by other denominations.

Seventh-day Adventist members have studied their Bibles and are convinced of the importance of their beliefs. Therefore, they will often share Bible texts, booklets, tracts, videos, or other materials that communicate their point of view with others. So you shouldn't find it unusual if a Seventh-day Adventist hands you a book or pamphlet that further describes some especially meaningful doctrine. Perhaps a Seventh-day Adventist sent you this book or handed it to you at home or work.

Seventh-day Adventists feel convinced that they have a clear but fragmentary understanding of how God has worked in the past, how He guides in the present, and what He plans to do in the future. This brings the peace of Christ to their lives. As a result of their understanding of God's care, providence, and plans for tomorrow, they typically display a great deal of hope, even amid tragedy. In this world of turmoil Seventh-day Adventists are delighted to share the hope and peace they have discovered in God's Word.

Seventh-day Adventist members around the world hold the same fundamental religious beliefs. (See Appendix B.) The church in Korea does not teach doctrine different from the church in Sweden. Because Seventh-day Adventists are a *worldwide* group of believers, their belief in God and His Word transcends cultural and ethnic barriers, which, of course, encourages unity.

As mentioned previously, Seventh-day Adventists believe that each person is valuable in God's eyes. This belief is translated into action in two ways.

First, it paves the way for unity in the worldwide church. When Seventh-day Adventists gather together for a meeting, race, nationality, or ethnic diversity is not a relevant issue. Blacks and Whites, Chinese and Russians, Iranians and Israelis, will fellowship together as brothers and sisters because of Christ.

Second, it shapes the way they relate to each other

and to the world around them. You'll find Seventh-day Adventists assisting low-income families, providing relief to starving children, holding the hand of an AIDS patient, or delivering a meal to an elderly widow. Seventh-day Adventists try to follow Christ's example of caring for others.

Seventh-day Adventists are thoughtful about the things they do. You'll presumably not hear them swearing or using God's name lightly. They believe they represent to others what Christ is like. They are careful to try to do those things that would please Him. It's worth emphasizing again that Seventh-day Adventists don't attempt good behavior in order to be saved, but because they've experienced God's saving grace.

It's customary for many Seventh-day Adventists to set apart some time during the day to read their Bibles or do some further study on a Scripture passage. They also dedicate time each day to pray, realizing that prayer is a vital part of any Christian's life. If you've ever been around Seventh-day Adventists at mealtime, you may have observed them bowing their heads to thank God for their food. This simple act is an acknowledgment of God's goodness.

Speaking of food, Seventh-day Adventists are conscientious about what they eat. They believe their bodies are temples of the Holy Spirit, and they desire to treat them with respect. Many Seventh-day Adventists have chosen a vegetarian diet. This is, in part, a logical consequence of their belief that the most healthful foods are those God originally gave us to eat in Eden—fruits, nuts, grains, and vegetables. And those Seventh-day Adventists who aren't vegetarians generally don't consume large quantities of meat.

Many members exercise regularly, trying to stay physically fit.

Seventh-day Adventists believe they shouldn't subject their bodies to any known substances that would be harmful. They avoid using such things as mind-altering illegal drugs, alcohol, or cigarettes.

Demographic and epidemiological research has shown that the average Seventh-day Adventist lives seven years longer than average.

Seventh-day Adventists will most likely be selective about the kind of entertainment they engage in and use scriptural principles to determine their choices. Some may simply ask themselves the question Would Jesus participate in such an activity? Seventh-day Adventists try to fill their minds with quality material, whether it be reading matter, television programs, or radio shows.

You might find that most Seventh-day Adventists aren't into high fashion, because many members desire simplicity of lifestyle. This philosophy helps to guide their selection of what they wear, how they spend their money, and how they prioritize their lives.

Some Seventh-day Adventists have risen in their fields to make some outstanding contributions because of their personal commitment to follow Christ and biblical principles. I could share some names of Seventh-day Adventists whom you'd readily recognize. They've been acknowledged by kings and presidents. Others have won awards and commendations. However, the majority of Seventh-day Adventists do not receive public honor but quietly live for Christ—and others. They share hope in the workplace, filling needs where these are felt, being productive citizens in their local communities, and adding joy to a world cursed with suffering.

My words may sound like a rosy portrayal of a perfect group of people. It might seem that way, but all of us live in a world of mistakes, flaws, and errors. Seventh-day Adventists have their faults too. Although the things I've described are the ideals members strive for, they sometimes (even often) fall short of these high standards. When they do stumble, Seventh-day Adventists accept the forgiveness that God offers and continue their quest to lead a life in harmony with the wishes of the great Lawgiver of the universe.

How do Seventh-day Adventists maintain their organization? How does the denomination continue to grow and flourish? How do they worship together and share with others? Let's discover more about this in the next chapter.

CHAPTER 4

What Is the Seventh-day Adventist Church Like?

DURING THE LATTER PART of 1998 the NASDAQ Combined Composite Index began a steady climb upward. As the tech-heavy index rose month after month, many analysts ignored historical data and proclaimed this was the beginning of the "New Economy." Daytraders became legends. New investors flooded the market with cash in the hopes of striking it rich on the most innovative dot.coms. The index continued its breathtaking climb, and on March 9, 2000, closed at over 5,000—an incredible 18-month performance.

While many euphoric investors made plans for early retirement and luxury purchases, a minority of analysts had been predicting a coming burst in what they called the "Internet bubble." Those who listened to their message redirected their money into bonds and money market funds in order to protect their assets. The prediction came true. The NASDAQ reversed its course and began to plunge. In late 2002 the index sank to a year low of 1,139—a low that had not been seen since 1996. With the exception of the occasional time we may throw caution to the wind and take a calculated risk, most of us actually prefer the familiar and comfortable. We try to avoid the unknown and the unexpected. Although we've all taken risks at one time or another—such as making an investment, starting a new career, or moving to a new location—most of us feel much more secure when we know what to expect.

You might recall the feelings you experienced as a child on your first day of school. Would the teacher be nice? Would the other kids treat you kindly? Would you be able to find your way around the big school building? You didn't know what to expect. You might recollect a nauseous feeling in your stomach, your damp palms, and your pounding heart. Those feelings all served as a reminder that you were entering unfamiliar territory.

Some people have never visited any church other than the one in which they were raised. Perhaps they haven't had that desire because they don't know what to expect. If they considered making a visit, a number of questions might arise in their minds: Will they lock the doors and not let me out until I join the church? Will I find dancing, pew-hopping, or brainwashing? Will there be crystals, chants, or séances?

I can't answer for every church, but let me try to give you as much information as I can in this short space about your local Seventh-day Adventist church. Then when you visit, it will be more like the familiar and comfortable than the unknown and unexpected.

Seventh-day Adventist churches around the world vary somewhat in liturgy, music, and format. You may hear an organ in New England, a banjo in Tennessee, a drum in Mozambique, or a zither in China. There may be smiles and hand-clapping in one congregation and more solemn faces in another. Congregations can be very large or as small as 10 or 20 members.

But whatever the variances, there's one thing you can expect in every Seventh-day Adventist church you attend around the world. You'll find friendly, Christian people—people who will be happy you've taken the time to come and worship the Lord with them.

In most Seventh-day Adventist churches the Saturday morning service is divided into two parts. The first part is called Sabbath school, which offers age-appropriate classes for children, as well as various classes for adults. From infancy children learn about Jesus' saving love. Lively songs, creative Bible stories, hands-on activities, and caring teachers demonstrate the joy of knowing Christ. The adults also learn more about God and His Word as church members and guests study together a specific biblical topic or Scripture passage. A majority of Seventh-day Adventist churches uses the same Bible curriculum for study.

The second part of the service is the worship portion. Usually the whole church meets together during this time. Although the preliminaries may vary, some basic elements can be found in most Seventh-day Adventist worship services. There will be time to join in congregational worship and praise, such as singing hymns, sharing prayer requests, or giving "testimonies." The sermon typically deals with a topic of Scripture relevant to the needs of the members, focusing on the church's mission and message. The sermon may be delivered by the local pastor or a designated speaker in the pastor's absence.

Everyone voluntarily participates in any portion of the church service as desired. There's no coercion, no locked doors, and no burly deacons guarding the entrance. What you will find when you visit a Seventh-day Adventist church is a group of Christians who are happy to be together. They've come to church in order to share and learn, to be refreshed and encouraged for another week of living in a sin-struck world.

The pastor is not paid by the local church, but rather by the area "conference." Such a practice enables the pastor to preach to the hearts of the people, rather than to their "pocketbooks." A policy unique to the Seventh-day Adventist denomination is to pay local pastors on the same wage scale whether they minister to a congregation of 50 or 5,000, thus eliminating much of the competitiveness so prevalent in society. It reduces the desire to climb the ladder, so to speak.

You might know where the Seventh-day Adventist church is located in your town or city. Although the building is what's most visible in the community, the organization is much broader. The members of your local Seventh-day Adventist church actually have a representative voice in the collective body of the world church. Let's take a look at how the denomination does its business.

In 1863 the Seventh-day Adventist Church had completed all the steps necessary for official organization. Some adjustments have been effected since then, but the main organizational structure still exists. You see, the principles that helped to form the church have also helped to maintain its integrity through the years.

The foundation of the Seventh-day Adventist Church is its members. Any person who has accepted Jesus Christ as personal Saviour and understands and adheres to the common beliefs of Seventh-day Adventists can join the church. These individual members, as a collective voice, have input into the world church. Because they are guided by the principles in the Word of God, there are no uprisings or drastic departures from the beliefs or policies that have directed the church in the past.

Individual members of the local church elect representatives from their congregations to meet together and select local "conference" officers. The local conference embraces an area usually about the size of a state. For example, some local conferences are the Pennsylvania Conference, Michigan Conference, and Carolina Conference. The local conferences manage affairs within their jurisdiction and provide facilities and programs that directly affect the individual church members in that area.

Local conferences are grouped together, just as the local churches are, to form "union conferences." The unions are made up of specific geographic regions, and the officers of these unions oversee church-related work in those areas. There are nine such unions in North America, such as the Southern Union, Atlantic Union, and Pacific Union.

This same pattern of distributing responsibility continues. The unions are grouped together to form "divisions" of the General Conference. Thirteen divisions span the globe, such as the North American Division, Southern Asia Division, and Euro-Africa Division. Currently the largest divisions in the Seventh-day Adventist Church are the East-Central Africa, Inter-America, and South America. Each of these Divisions has a membership exceeding 2 million. The divisions are all represented in the "General Conference," whose ultimate responsibility is to encourage, lead, manage, and direct the Seventh-day Adventist Church around the world. The General Conference world headquarters is located in Silver Spring, Maryland.

The biblical foundation for the organization of the Seventh-day Adventist Church is found in Exodus 18. This passage reveals that Moses was instructed to divide his workload and distribute responsibility among the people of Israel. More than 100 years of following these same guidelines has proved this to be an effective means of enabling the Seventh-day Adventist Church to carry out its worldwide mission.

The organizational structure that the Seventh-day Adventist Church adopted has enabled it to expand from a total of 132 organizations in 1863 to more than 60,000 today! It has permitted the church to grow from 30 paid employees to more than 190,000! It has also enabled the church to increase from 3,500 baptized church members to more than 13 million today! Under God's blessing, the organizational structure has indeed helped to facilitate the Seventh-day Adventist Church in pursuing its mission.

But exactly what is the mission of the Seventh-day Adventist Church? What are the members trying to accomplish? How is the church fulfilling its mission? What drives the members to give, work, share, and dedicate themselves to service? Let's look at the final chapter for an answer to these questions.

CHAPTER 5

What Is the Seventh-day Adventist Mission?

IN MAY OF 1961 PRESIDENT John F. Kennedy initiated the Apollo space program. It was born with one mission in mind—before the end of the decade the nation should place a person on the moon and get them home again. A full-scale offensive was begun to fulfill this purpose. The program had skeptics, trials and errors, and even major setbacks. For example, in 1967 fire broke out during a launchpad test, and three American astronauts died in its flames. The tragedy threw the whole space program into question. But despite all the failures, and without the presence of the president who had created the vision for the American people, on July 20, 1969, the world watched in amazement as Neil Armstrong stepped out of the tiny space module of Apollo 11 and planted his feet on the surface of the moon. With the astronauts' safe return to earth, the mission was accomplished!

People are mission-driven. Whether it be as small as weeding the garden or as big as landing on the moon, people will go to great lengths to fulfill a mission. Countries, cities, families, individuals, and churches have missions. Seventh-day Adventists also have a mission.

The Seventh-day Adventist mission is simply to teach people of all nations the "everlasting gospel" of Jesus and the commandments of God. It's based on the Great Commission given by Christ and recorded in Matthew 28:19, 20. Seventh-day Adventists actively study and teach the word of Scripture. They not only teach the Word, but also attempt to demonstrate its principles through acts of compassion. Every organization that is set up within the Seventh-day Adventist Church, every school that is started, every hospital opened, every church built, is done with the express purpose of fulfilling the mission of the church.

So, what methods do Seventh-day Adventists use to accomplish their mission? Any and all that are in harmony with Scripture! It would be impossible to describe each entity that is financially sponsored by the church or all the personal ministries that are independently sponsored by caring Seventh-day Adventists. Following is a short description of a few of the many methods and organizations that are being utilized by the church to fulfill its mission.

Mission Service—Since 1874, when J. N. Andrews left the United States to share the gospel of Christ in Europe, Seventh-day Adventists have recognized the importance of missions. Today the church has a multifaceted mission program.

Global Mission is one Seventh-day Adventist organization sharing the everlasting gospel of Jesus and teaching the commandments of God in areas of the world that have not heard this wonderful news. The focus of Global Mission is on specific people groups, languages, and dialects rather than entire countries. Dedicated men and women, assigned to a specific ministry area, share their faith whenever the opportunity arises. Since its inception in 1990, Global Mission has entered more than 8,000 of the 15,000 areas targeted for outreach.

Numerous other programs and organizations also provide opportunity for sharing the gospel. Young Pioneers seeks to utilize the talents of youth in mission service. Maranatha Flights International harnesses the energies of volunteers, who travel to various locations around the world to build churches for those who need them. Adventists have many other diverse opportunities for long-term or short-term mission service within the church. Each one provides members an avenue for sharing their time, talents, and faith.

Relief and Development—Seventh-day Adventists understand that sharing the gospel of Christ means more than just preaching. Christ often ministered to the physical needs of people before He met their spiritual ones. The church's relief and development ministries focus primarily on meeting the physical needs of people.

Adventist Development and Relief Agency (ADRA) is an enormous organization unselfishly making the world a better place to live. Its main purpose is to do individual and community development and to provide disaster relief in times of tragedy. ADRA workers believe that each life is infinitely valuable. They try to improve standards of living, especially in deprived areas of the world.

ADRA is presently working in 143 countries. Current emphasis involves disaster relief, education, food programs, and health and water projects. Whenever you hear or read of a major disaster, you can be certain that ADRA is on the way to that location or is already there to assist. When the destruction caused by a disaster has been cleared, ADRA doesn't pack up and leave. It makes a long-term commitment to enhance the quality of life for the survivors. In this respect, ADRA uniquely demonstrates the principles of Christ to the world.

Education—Seventh-day Adventists believe in improving the whole person spiritually, physically, and mentally. Early in Seventh-day Adventist history the need for church-sponsored schools was realized. Today the Seventh-day Adventist Church has one of the largest private parochial educational systems in the world, with more than 6,000 schools and a combined enrollment of more than 1 million students. The church also operates a number of colleges and universities, including Home Study International, which provides an accredited home-study program.

Health Care—Many Seventh-day Adventists venture to use their God-given talents in healing people with the aid of medical knowledge available today and as led by the Spirit of the Lord. For this reason the church operates over 725 hospitals, clinics, senior centers, and children's homes around the world, employing more than 75,000 people. Many patients have been drawn closer to the Lord as they have experienced the care given by Christian medical personnel. Thus hospital employees are making a contribution in fulfilling the mission of the church.

Many Seventh-day Adventist medical personnel in developed countries dedicate their talents to the citizens of economically deprived countries. One such group of volunteers is the heart specialty team based at Loma Linda University Medical Center, a denominationally sponsored hospital. The team provides advanced life-saving medical procedures to people who otherwise could not afford this service.

Proclaiming the Word—The Seventh-day Adventist mission could not be fulfilled if it were not for a distinctive proclamation of the everlasting gospel of Jesus and the commandments of God. The church uses various means to accomplish this. In addition to evangelists, pastors, and Bible instructors, there are also radiobroadcasts, television transmissions, and a publishing work to help fulfill that mission.

The *It Is Written* weekly television program, founded in 1956, has proclaimed the Word of God across continents and has been translated into many languages. *It Is Written* teaches the Bible through its Web site (www.written.org) and through worldwide satellite broadcasts, available in thousands of locations and reaching millions of people.

Adventist World Radio is a ministry using the airwaves for evangelism. Its broadcasts have blanketed much of the world with the everlasting gospel. With its humble beginnings on October 1, 1971, Adventist World Radio now presents Bible truth in more than 50 languages. With its combined programming, AWR is on the air more than 1,200 hours a week.

The Seventh-day Adventist Church operates 55 publishing houses and currently offers material in 343 different languages and dialects. More than 6,000 "literature evangelists" sell and distribute this material that teaches about Jesus and His Word.

With this brief overview we have just begun to scratch the surface in describing how Seventh-day Adventists go about fulfilling their mission. From this summary I believe you can see they are serious about sharing the everlasting gospel of Jesus and teaching the commandments of God.

Have these diversified approaches worked? You be the judge. In 1863 the Seventh-day Adventist Church had a baptized membership of 3,500. By 1960 the membership had risen to more than 1 million. By 1980 it had topped 3 million. In 1990 there were more than 6 million members. By the year 2003 membership had grown to more than 13 million. Today the church is adding more than a million members every year. A new member is baptized into the Seventh-day Adventist Church an average of every 30 seconds. New churches are being established at the rate of one every five hours. The church currently has organized work in more than 200 of the 230 countries and areas of the world. This is more than any other Protestant denomination has.

You could say that the Seventh-day Adventist Church is not just a denomination; it's a movement. It's a movement of people who are eager to obey God's commands, to stay true to His Word, and to follow His plan for their lives.

Seventh-day Adventists happily share the principles of His kingdom with others. They desire to live their own lives as a demonstration of Christ's character. People from any race, creed, ethnic origin, background, or religion are invited into the fellowship of the Seventh-day Adventist Church. And seeing people accept Jesus Christ and His Word is what helps to keep the mission alive!

Before You Finish . . .

EVEN THOUGH WE LIVE in the information age, those just learning about Seventh-day Adventists may read this book and think they have been overloaded with too much information. On the other hand, someone who is well acquainted with Seventh-day Adventists may wish I had discussed certain aspects in more depth. Whatever the case, I hope now you have a little better picture of this group of Christian believers who worship Jesus and go to church on Saturday.

Maybe as you read this book, you actually thought—as others have—that Seventh-day Adventism makes a lot of sense. Perhaps as you more closely examine the beliefs of Seventh-day Adventists, found in the Appendices, you'll feel these tenets answer questions you've had.

Maybe believing in a God who puts a final end to sin makes a lot more sense to you than believing in a God who tortures people with scorching fire for millions and billions of years. Maybe believing in a God who will resurrect His people at the soon coming of Christ makes a lot more sense than believing in one who takes people to heaven at death, where they can later be reunited with their bodies. Maybe believing in a God who has a real place prepared for us in heaven makes more sense to you than believing in a God who will give you a harp and have you sit on a cloud for eternity as some airy ghost. Maybe believing in a God who still asks you to keep the seventh day of the week as His Sabbath, which He ordained at Creation, makes more sense than believing in a God who would change the rules during the middle of the game. If this is the case, then maybe you'd like to take a closer look at what Seventh-day Adventists believe.

If you were just perusing this book for curiosity's sake, I trust you now have a clearer picture of Seventh-day Adventists. I hope you see that they are a deeply spiritual people who love the Lord Jesus Christ and who realize that their only hope of salvation comes through Him. I hope you see that they are students of the Bible and try to do the Lord's will. I hope you see that Seventh-day Adventists are not some confused extremists, but sincere followers of God.

Whatever the case and for whatever reason you read this, the next time someone asks, "Who are the Seventh-day Adventists?" I hope you'll be there to offer them a correct response!

APPENDIX A

A Brief Scriptural Summary of Selected Seventh-day Adventist Beliefs

LISTED BELOW IS A BRIEF scriptural study of selected Seventh-day Adventist beliefs. For a more complete study on these topics, contact your local Seventh-day Adventist church, which will be happy to supply you with more information.

Acceptance and Forgiveness in Christ

Romans 3:23 says that everyone on earth has made mistakes—has sinned.

Romans 3:10 says that there is no one on earth who is righteous.

John 3:16, 17 says that God offers eternal life to anyone who believes.

Acts 4:12 says that there is salvation only through Christ.

Ephesians 2:8, 9 says that we are saved by grace, not works.

Romans 6:23 says that we deserve death, but God offers the gift of life.

First John 1:9 says that if we confess our sins, God will forgive them.

Revelation 3:20 says that His invitation is open to all who will believe.

Second Coming of Christ

John 14:1-3 says that Jesus promised He would return to earth.

Matthew 24:3-7 says that many signs will take place prior to Christ's coming.

Matthew 24:14 says that the gospel will be preached in all the world before Jesus comes.

Revelation 1:7 says that when Jesus returns, everyone will see Him.

Matthew 24:27 says that His return will not be a secret event.

First Thessalonians 4:16, 17 says that the righteous dead will be resurrected at Christ's return.

Revelation 6:14-17 says that those who have not accepted Christ fear His coming.

Titus 2:13 says that Jesus' soon coming is a hope to many people.

The Law of God

Deuteronomy 6:5 and *Leviticus 19:18* say that the two great laws of the Old Testament are love for God and love for your neighbor.

Romans 3:20 says that we are not justified by keeping the law, but that the law points out our sin.

First John 3:4 says that sin is actually breaking God's law.

John 14:15 says that if we love God, we will keep His commandments.

Revelation 12:17 and *Revelation 14:12* say that God's faithful people at the end of time will keep all the commandments of God.

The Sabbath

Genesis 2:1-3 says that the seventh-day Sabbath (Saturday) was created in the Garden of Eden.

Revelation 14:6, 7 says that in the last days God calls us to worship Him as the Creator.

Exodus 20:8-11 says that the seventh-day Sabbath is given as a commandment and as a sign of God's creative power.

Luke 4:16 says that Jesus kept the Sabbath.

Acts 13:42-44 says that Paul kept the Sabbath.

Isaiah 66:22, 23 says that in heaven we will keep the Sabbath.

> How do we know for sure that Saturday is the same Sabbath Jesus kept? Jesus died on the preparation day (Friday), He rose on the first day of the week (Sunday), and the day He was in the tomb was called the Sabbath (Saturday). (See Luke 23:54-56; 24:1.)

Revelation 14:12 says that the saints of God are commandment keepers.

Revelation 12:17 says that the devil is angry with

those who keep God's commandments.

Daniel 7:25 predicted that an earthly power would try to change God's laws.

The State of the Dead

In *John 11:11-14* Jesus compares death to sleep.

Genesis 2:7 says that body + breath = a living soul.

Ecclesiastes 12:7 says that at death the body returns to the ground and the breath returns to God, and the soul ceases to exist.

Psalm 146:3, 4 says that when people die they have no more thoughts.

Psalm 115:17 says that the dead don't praise God.

Ecclesiastes 9:5 says that the dead do not know anything.

First Thessalonians 4:15, 16 says that at the second coming of Jesus the righteous dead will be resurrected from their graves.

The Destruction of the Wicked

Second Peter 3:9 says that God does not want anyone to perish.

John 3:16, 17 says that God offers eternal life to all who believe.

Psalm 37:20 says that those who reject God will ultimately be destroyed.

Malachi 4:1-3 says that sinners will be completely destroyed and turned to ashes.

Revelation 20:9 says that fire will ultimately destroy the wicked.

Revelation 21:1-5 says that God will create all things

new after all the sinners have been destroyed, and all the former things will have passed away.

Heaven and the New Earth

John 14:1-3 says that heaven is a very real place, with real people and things.

Revelation 21:3 says that God will dwell with us.

Hebrews 11:10 says that Abraham looked forward to going to heaven.

Isaiah 65:21 says that we will be able to build homes and plant crops in the new earth.

Isaiah 66:23 says that we will come together to worship the Lord on Sabbath.

Revelation 21:4 says that there will be no more death, sorrow, crying, or pain there.

Revelation 22:3 says that we will serve the Lord with joy!

Earth's Last Message

Revelation 14:6-12 says that three messages are to be given to the world prior to Jesus' coming.

Revelation 14:6, 7 says that the first angel's message is one that will be given to the whole world. It is a message describing the judgment in heaven. It also is a call to worship the Creator, an act that is carried out by worshiping God on His Sabbath, which is given as a memorial of His creative power.

Revelation 14:8 says that the second angel's message announces the fall of Babylon. Babylon symbolizes apostasy against God and His truth.

The fall of Babylon is a description of those

> individuals or churches that compromise Scripture for the sake of their own comfort, rather than following God's Word.

Revelation 14:9-11 says that the third angel's message is a message of warning to beware of receiving the mark of the beast.

> The beast power sets up laws in opposition to God's laws and commands people to obey them. According to Revelation 13:3, this power is a popular religious system that is admired by much of the world. Those who willingly choose to follow this system of worship, in contrast to those who worship the Creator as He requests, receive the mark of the beast.

Revelation 14:12 says that God's people are those who keep all the commandments of God and have the simple faith of Jesus.

Revelation 14:4 says that those faithful to God will follow Jesus wherever He leads them.

APPENDIX B

27 Fundamental Beliefs of Seventh-day Adventists

THE FOLLOWING IS THE SEVENTH-DAY Adventist Church's official statement of beliefs, as adopted by its members. For a further biblical study on any of these beliefs, please contact your local Seventh-day Adventist church. Someone there will be happy to supply you with that information.

1. The Holy Scriptures

The Holy Scriptures, Old and New Testaments, are the written Word of God, given by divine inspiration through holy men of God who spoke and wrote as they were moved by the Holy Spirit. In this Word, God has committed to man the knowledge necessary for salvation. The Holy Scriptures are the infallible revelation of His will. They are the standard of character, the test of experience, the authoritative revealer of doctrines, and the trustworthy record of God's acts in history.

2. The Trinity

There is one God: Father, Son, and Holy Spirit, a unity of three co-eternal Persons. God is immortal, all-powerful, all-knowing, above all, and ever present. He is infinite and beyond human comprehension, yet known through His self-revelation. He is forever worthy of worship, adoration, and service by the whole creation.

3. The Father

God the eternal Father is the Creator, Source, Sustainer, and Sovereign of all creation. He is just and holy, merciful and gracious, slow to anger, and abounding in steadfast love and faithfulness. The qualities and powers exhibited in the Son and the Holy Spirit are also revelations of the Father.

4. The Son

God the eternal Son became incarnate in Jesus Christ. Through Him all things were created, the character of God is revealed, the salvation of humanity is accomplished, and the world is judged. Forever truly God, He became also truly man, Jesus the Christ. He was conceived of the Holy Spirit and born of the virgin Mary. He lived and experienced temptation as a human being, but perfectly exemplified the righteousness and love of God. By His miracles He manifested God's power and was attested as God's promised Messiah. He suffered and died voluntarily on the cross for our sins and in our place, was raised from the dead, and ascended to minister in the heavenly sanctuary in our behalf. He will come again in glory for the final deliverance of His people and the restoration of all things.

5. The Holy Spirit

God the eternal Spirit was active with the Father and the Son in Creation, incarnation, and redemption. He inspired the writers of Scripture. He filled Christ's life with power. He draws and convicts human beings; and those who respond He renews and transforms into the image of God. Sent by the Father and the Son to be always with His children, He extends spiritual gifts to the church, empowers it to bear witness to Christ, and in harmony with the Scriptures leads it into all truth.

6. Creation

God is Creator of all things, and has revealed in Scripture the authentic account of His creative activity. In six days the Lord made "the heaven and the earth" and all living things upon the earth, and rested on the seventh day of that first week. Thus He established the Sabbath as a perpetual memorial of His completed creative work. The first man and woman were made in the image of God as the crowning work of Creation, given dominion over the world, and charged with responsibility to care for it. When the world was finished it was "very good," declaring the glory of God.

7. The Nature of Man

Man and woman were made in the image of God with individuality, the power and freedom to think and to do. Though created free beings, each is an indivisible unity of body, mind, and spirit, dependent upon God for life and breath and all else. When our first parents disobeyed God, they denied their dependence upon Him and fell from their high position under God. The image of God in them was marred and they became subject to death. Their descendants share this fallen nature and its consequences. They are born with weaknesses and tendencies to evil. But God in Christ reconciled the world to Himself and by His Spirit restores in penitent mortals the image of their Maker. Created for the glory of God, they are called to love Him and one another, and to care for their environment.

8. The Great Controversy

All humanity is now involved in a great controversy between Christ and Satan regarding the character of God, His law, and His sovereignty over the universe. This conflict originated in heaven when a created being, endowed with freedom of choice, in self-exaltation became Satan, God's adversary, and led into rebellion a portion of the angels. He introduced the spirit of rebellion into this world when he led Adam and Eve into sin. This human sin resulted in the distortion of the image of God in humanity, the disordering of the created world, and its eventual devastation at the time of the worldwide flood. Observed by the whole creation, this world became the arena of the universal conflict, out of which the God of love will ultimately be vindicated. To assist His people in this controversy, Christ sends the Holy Spirit and the loyal angels to guide, protect, and sustain them in the way of salvation.

9. The Life, Death, and Resurrection of Christ

In Christ's life of perfect obedience to God's will, His suffering, death, and resurrection, God provided the only means of atonement for human sin, so that those who by faith accept this atonement may have eternal life, and the whole creation may better understand the infinite and holy love of the Creator. This perfect atonement vindicates the righteousness of God's law and the graciousness of His character; for it both condemns our sin and provides for our forgiveness. The death of Christ is substitutionary and expiatory, reconciling and transforming. The resurrection of Christ proclaims God's triumph over the forces of evil, and for those who accept the atonement assures their final victory over sin and death. It declares the Lordship of Jesus Christ, before whom every knee in heaven and on earth will bow.

10. The Experience of Salvation

In infinite love and mercy God made Christ, who knew no sin, to be sin for us, so that in Him we might be made the righteousness of God. Led by the Holy Spirit we sense our need, acknowledge our sinfulness, repent of our transgressions, and exercise faith in Jesus as Lord and Christ, as Substitute and Example. This faith which receives salvation comes through the divine power of the Word and is the gift of God's grace. Through Christ we are justified, adopted as God's sons and daughters, and delivered from the lordship of sin. Through the Spirit we are born again and sanctified; the Spirit renews our minds, writes God's law of love in our hearts, and we are given the power to live a holy life. Abiding in Him we become partakers of the divine nature and have the assurance of salvation now and in the judgment.

11. The Church

The church is the community of believers who confess Jesus Christ as Lord and Saviour. In continuity with the people of God in Old Testament times, we are called out from the world; and we join together for worship, for fellowship, for instruction in the Word, for the celebration of the Lord's Supper, for service to all mankind, and for the worldwide proclamation of the gospel. The church derives its authority from Christ, who is the incarnate Word, and from the Scriptures, which are the written Word. The church is God's family; adopted by Him as children, its members live on the basis of the new covenant. The church is the body of Christ, a community of faith of which Christ Himself is the Head. The church is the bride for whom Christ died that He might sanctify and cleanse her. At His return in triumph, He will present her to Himself a glorious church, the faithful of all the ages, the purchase of His blood, not having spot or wrinkle, but holy and without blemish.

12. The Remnant and Its Mission

The universal church is composed of all who truly believe in Christ, but in the last days, a time of widespread apostasy, a remnant has been called out to keep the commandments of God and the faith of

Jesus. This remnant announces the arrival of the judgment hour, proclaims salvation through Christ, and heralds the approach of His second advent. This proclamation is symbolized by the three angels of Revelation 14; it coincides with the work of judgment in heaven and results in a work of repentance and reform on earth. Every believer is called to have a personal part in this worldwide witness.

13. Unity in the Body of Christ

The church is one body with many members, called from every nation, kindred, tongue, and people. In Christ we are a new creation; distinctions of race, culture, learning, and nationality, and differences between high and low, rich and poor, male and female, must not be divisive among us. We are all equal in Christ, who by one Spirit has bonded us into one fellowship with Him and with one another; we are to serve and be served without partiality or reservation. Through the revelation of Jesus Christ in the Scriptures we share the same faith and hope, and reach out in one witness to all. This unity has its source in the oneness of the triune God, who has adopted us as His children.

14. Baptism

By baptism we confess our faith in the death and resurrection of Jesus Christ, and testify of our death to sin and of our purpose to walk in newness of life. Thus we acknowledge Christ as Lord and Saviour, become His people, and are received as members by His church. Baptism is a symbol of our union with Christ, the forgiveness of our sins, and our reception of the Holy Spirit. It is by immersion in water and is contingent on an affirmation of faith in Jesus and evidence of repentance of sin. It follows instruction in the Holy Scriptures and acceptance of their teachings.

15. The Lord's Supper

The Lord's Supper is a participation in the emblems of the body and blood of Jesus as an expression of faith in Him, our Lord and Saviour. In this experience of communion Christ is present to meet and strengthen His people. As we partake, we joyfully proclaim the Lord's death until He comes again. Preparation for the Supper includes self-examination, repentance, and confession. The Master ordained the service of foot washing to signify renewed cleansing, to express a willingness to serve one another in Christlike humility, and to unite our hearts in love. The Communion service is open to all believing Christians.

16. Spiritual Gifts and Ministries

God bestows upon all members of His church in every age spiritual gifts which each member is to employ in loving ministry for the common good of the church and of humanity. Given by the agency of the Holy Spirit, who apportions to each member as He wills, the gifts provide all abilities and ministries needed by the church to fulfill its divinely ordained functions. According to the Scriptures, these gifts include such ministries as faith, healing, prophecy, proclamation, teaching, administration, reconciliation, compassion, and self-sacrificing service and charity for the help and encouragement of people. Some members are called of God and endowed by the Spirit for functions recognized by the church in pastoral, evangelistic, apostolic, and teaching ministries particularly needed to equip the members for service, to build up the church to spiritual maturity, and to foster unity of the faith and knowledge of God. When members employ these spiritual gifts as faithful stewards of God's varied grace, the church is protected from the destructive influence of false doctrine, grows with a growth that is from God, and is built up in faith and love.

17. The Gift of Prophecy

One of the gifts of the Holy Spirit is prophecy. This gift is an identifying mark of the remnant church and was manifested in the ministry of Ellen G. White. As the Lord's messenger, her writings are a continuing and authoritative source of truth which provide for the church comfort, guidance, instruction, and correction. They also make clear that the Bible is the standard by which all teaching and experience must be tested.

18. The Law of God

The great principles of God's law are embodied in the Ten Commandments and exemplified in the life of Christ. They express God's love, will, and purposes concerning human conduct and relationships and are binding upon all people in every age. These precepts are the basis of God's covenant with His people and the standard in God's judgment. Through the agency of the Holy Spirit they point out sin and awaken a sense of need for a Saviour. Salvation is all of grace and not of works, but its fruitage is obedience to the Commandments. This obedience develops Christian character and results in a sense of well-being. It is an evidence of our love for the Lord and our concern for our fellow men. The obedience of faith demonstrates the power of Christ to transform lives, and therefore strengthens Christian witness.

19. The Sabbath

The beneficent Creator, after the six days of Creation, rested on the seventh day and instituted the Sabbath for all people as a memorial of Creation. The fourth commandment of God's unchangeable law requires the observance of this seventh-day Sabbath as the day of rest, worship, and ministry in harmony with the teaching and practice of Jesus, the Lord of the Sabbath. The Sabbath is a day of delightful communion with God and one another. It is a symbol of our redemption in Christ, a sign of our sanctification, a token of our allegiance, and a foretaste of our eternal future in God's kingdom. The Sabbath is God's perpetual sign of His eternal covenant between Him and His people. Joyful observance of this holy time from evening to evening, sunset to sunset, is a celebration of God's creative and redemptive acts.

20. Stewardship

We are God's stewards, entrusted by Him with time and opportunities, abilities and possessions, and the blessings of the earth and its resources. We are responsible to Him for their proper use. We acknowledge God's ownership by faithful service to Him and our fellowmen, and by returning tithes and giving offerings for the proclamation of His gospel and the support and growth of His church. Stewardship is a privilege given to us by God for nurture in love and the victory over selfishness and covetousness. The steward rejoices in the blessings that come to others as a result of his faithfulness.

21. Christian Behavior

We are called to be a godly people who think, feel, and act in harmony with the principles of heaven. For the Spirit to recreate in us the character of our Lord we involve ourselves only in those things which will produce Christlike purity, health, and joy in our lives. This means that our amusement and entertainment should meet the highest standards of Christian taste and beauty. While recognizing cultural differences, our dress is to be simple, modest, and neat, befitting those whose true beauty does not consist of outward adornment but in the imperishable ornament of a gentle and quiet spirit. It also means that because our bodies are the temples of the Holy Spirit, we are to care for them intelligently. Along with adequate exercise and rest, we are to adopt the most healthful diet possible and abstain from the unclean foods identified in the Scriptures. Since alcoholic beverages, tobacco, and the irresponsible use of drugs and narcotics are harmful to our bodies, we are to abstain from them as well. Instead, we are to engage in whatever brings our thoughts and bodies into the discipline of Christ, who desires our wholesomeness, joy, and goodness.

22. Marriage and the Family

Marriage was divinely established in Eden and affirmed by Jesus to be a lifelong union between a man and a woman in loving companionship. For the Christian a marriage commitment is to God as well as to the spouse, and should be entered into only between partners who share a common faith. Mutual love, honor, respect, and responsibility are the fabric of this relationship, which is to reflect the love, sanctity, closeness, and permanence of the relations[illegible] tween Christ and His church. Regarding divorce, Jesus taught that the person who divorces a spouse, except for fornication, and marries another, commits adultery. Although some family relationships may fall short of the ideal, marriage partners who fully commit themselves to each other in Christ may achieve loving unity through the guidance of the Spirit and the nurture of the church. God blesses the family and intends that its members shall assist each other toward complete maturity. Parents are to bring up their children to love and obey the Lord. By their example and their words they are to teach them that Christ is a loving disciplinarian, ever tender and caring, who wants them to become members of His body, the family of God. Increasing family closeness is one of the earmarks of the final gospel message.

23. Christ's Ministry in the Heavenly Sanctuary

There is a sanctuary in heaven, the true tabernacle which the Lord set up and not man. In it Christ ministers on our behalf, making available to believers the benefits of His atoning sacrifice offered once for all on the cross. He was inaugurated as our great High Priest and began His intercessory ministry at the time of His ascension. In 1844, at the end of the prophetic period of 2300 days, He entered the second and last phase of His atoning ministry. It is a work of investigative judgment which is part of the ultimate disposition of all sin, typified by the cleansing of the ancient Hebrew sanctuary on the Day of Atonement. In that typical service the sanctuary was cleansed with the blood of animal sacrifices, but the heavenly things are purified with the perfect sacrifice of the blood of Jesus. The investigative judgment reveals to heavenly intelligences who among the dead are asleep in Christ and therefore, in Him, are deemed worthy to have part in the first resurrection. It also makes manifest who among the living are abiding in Christ, keeping the commandments of God and the faith of Jesus, and in Him, therefore, are ready for translation into His everlasting kingdom. This judgment vindicates the justice of God in saving those who believe in Jesus. It declares that those who have remained loyal to God shall receive the kingdom. The completion of this ministry of Christ will mark the close of human probation before the Second Advent.

24. The Second Coming of Christ

The second coming of Christ is the blessed hope of

the church, the grand climax of the gospel. The Saviour's coming will be literal, personal, visible, and worldwide. When He returns, the righteous dead will be resurrected, and together with the righteous living will be glorified and taken to heaven, but the unrighteous will die. The almost complete fulfillment of most lines of prophecy, together with the present condition of the world, indicates that Christ's coming is imminent. The time of that event has not been revealed, and we are therefore exhorted to be ready at all times.

25. Death and Resurrection

The wages of sin is death. But God, who alone is immortal, will grant eternal life to His redeemed. Until that day death is an unconscious state for all people. When Christ, who is our life, appears, the resurrected righteous and the living righteous will be glorified and caught up to meet their Lord. The second resurrection, the resurrection of the unrighteous, will take place a thousand years later.

26. The Millennium and the End of Sin

The millennium is the thousand-year reign of Christ with His saints in heaven between the first and second resurrections. During this time the wicked dead will be judged; the earth will be utterly desolate, without living human inhabitants, but occupied by Satan and his angels. At its close Christ with His saints and the Holy City will descend from heaven to earth. The unrighteous dead will then be resurrected, and with Satan and his angels will surround the city; but fire from God will consume them and cleanse the earth. The universe will thus be freed of sin and sinners forever.

27. The New Earth

On the new earth, in which righteousness dwells, God will provide an eternal home for the redeemed and a perfect environment for everlasting life, love, joy, and learning in His presence. For here God Himself will dwell with His people, and suffering and death will have passed away. The great controversy will be ended, and sin will be no more. All things, animate and inanimate, will declare that God is love; and He shall reign forever. Amen.